Twenty to Make

Sugar Birds

Frances McNaughton

Search Press

First published in Great Britain 2011

Search Press Limited
Wellwood, North Farm Road,
Tunbridge Wells, Kent TN2 3DR

Text copyright © Frances McNaughton 2011

Photographs by Debbie Patterson at
Search Press Studios

Photographs and design copyright
© Search Press Ltd 2011

ISBN: 978-1-84448-672-4

Suppliers
If you have difficulty in obtaining any of the
materials and equipment mentioned in this book,
then please visit the Search Press website for
details of suppliers: www.searchpress.com

*This book is dedicated to my
Thursday Girls from Hawkhurst:
Margaret, Grace, Joyce, Linda, Rosemary
and Vera who have been my keenest
supporters since the early 1990s, and more
recently Holly and Gwen.*

Printed in Malaysia

Contents

Puffin

Materials:

25g (just under 1oz) black
   sugarpaste

Small pieces of white, orange,
   red, yellow and blue
   sugarpaste

Tools:

Heart cutter: 2.5cm (1in)

Small rolling pin

Dresden tool/cocktail stick

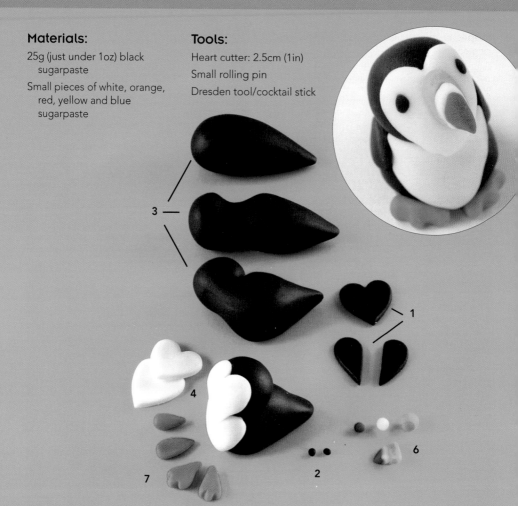

Instructions:

1 For the wings, roll out the black sugarpaste thinly.
Using the heart cutter, cut out the heart shape and then
cut it in half to make two wings.

2 For the eyes roll some black sugarpaste into two tiny balls.

3 Form the black sugarpaste into a 6cm (2½in) pointed cone for
the body. Roll gently between your two fingers at the rounded
end to make the neck and bend to stand the body up.

4 Roll out some white sugarpaste thinly. Using the heart cutter
again, cut out two hearts and stick on one for the tummy, and
one above it, slightly overlapping for the face.

5 Stick the two tiny black sugarpaste eyes and the wings in place.

6 Make a small pea-sized ball of blue sugarpaste, a smaller ball of yellow and an even smaller ball of red sugarpaste. Press them together to form the beak shape and stick the beak on to the head.

7 Roll two small pea-sized pieces of orange sugarpaste into cone shapes, and flatten slightly. Mark on three toes with the Dresden tool or a cocktail stick and attach them under the body.

Stick it on the Bill
Who could resist making this cute clown of the bird world?

Really Quick Penguin

Materials:

10g (¹/₃oz) white sugarpaste

10g (¹/₃oz) black sugarpaste

Small amount of yellow
   sugarpaste

Tools:

Square cutter: 2.5cm (1in)

No. 2 piping tube

2

3

1

Instructions:

1 Roll out the black sugarpaste. Make a tiny ball of yellow sugarpaste
and press it on to the black. Cut out a black square with the cutter, cutting
through the yellow on the corner of the square – this will form the beak.
Mark on two eyes with the piping tube.

2 For the Penguin's body, shape a cone from the white sugarpaste. The
length needs to be shorter than the diagonal of the square. Stand the cone
up on its base.

3 Cover the cone with the black sugarpaste square with the yellow beak
over the head first. The wings and tail can be left curved out or tweaked
until the model resembles a penguin!

P..P..P..Pick Up a Penguin!
These sweet treats are as cool as ice, and a piece of cake to make!

11

Stork

Materials:

White edible sugar candy stick

35g (1¼oz) white modelling paste (see page 6)

Small amounts of orange, black and pink or blue sugarpaste

Tools:

Dresden tool/ cocktail stick

Cutting wheel/ knife

Square cutter: 2.5cm (1in)

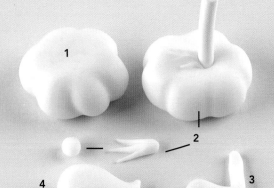

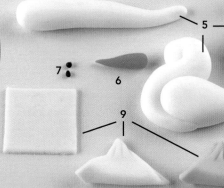

Instructions:

1 To model the cloud base, shape 25g (¾oz) of the white modelling paste with the Dresden tool. Make a hole with a dry candy stick in the centre of the top of the cloud where the leg will go.

2 To make one foot, take a small pea-sized 0.5cm (¼in) piece of white sugarpaste, shape it to a long cone and cut the pointed end into three points for the toes or claws. Attach this foot on top of the cloud in front of the leg hole. Dampen the end of the sugar candy stick and push it vertically into the cloud through the heel end of the foot. Push it right through to touch the bottom surface.

3 Make the second leg by rolling white modelling paste – measure it against the first leg and foot which are positioned on the cloud. Form the sausage shape into a point at the foot end. As before, cut the foot into three points for the toes or claws. Bend the knee pointing backwards, and the foot bending down. Dampen the standing stick at the top, attach the second leg and bend it into position sticking the ankle against the first leg. Allow it to dry, preferably overnight.

4 For the body you will need 5g (¼oz) of white modelling paste. Form a cone shape and turn the tail up slightly.

5 For the head and neck take 5g (¼oz) of white modelling paste. Make a carrot shape 6.5cm (2½in) long. Attach the narrow end of the carrot shape to the front of the body. Bend it to form a tight 'S' shape, dampening it if necessary to keep it in place.

6 To make the beak, roll a small pea-sized piece of orange sugarpaste to a tiny carrot shape 2cm (¾in) long. Stick the beak on, following the line of the neck.

7 Make two tiny black eyes by rolling two tiny balls of black sugarpaste and stick them on to the head.

8 Dampen the tops of the legs and stick the body on top, making sure it is balanced.

9 Roll blue or pink paste thinly and cut a 2.5cm (1in) square. Fold it diagonally and mark with two or three creases where the two points join. Stick it on to the end of the beak.

Bundle of Joy

This sweet stork is perfect to celebrate a new arrival – simply change the colour of the blanket for a new baby boy or baby girl.

Owl

Materials:

25g (just under 1oz) brown or chocolate sugarpaste

Small amounts of white, pale brown and black sugarpaste

Tools:

Small sharp-pointed scissors

Small sieve/sugarcraft gun

Heart cutter: 2.5cm (1in)

Circle cutters: 2cm (³/₄in) and 1cm (³/₈in)

Small rolling pin

Instructions:

1 To make the beak, form a tiny cone from brown sugarpaste.

2 For the two wings, model each from a large pea-sized piece of brown paste and make into a fat carrot shape. Flatten slightly and mark on the feathers using the Dresden tool.

3 To make the body, roll the main piece of brown sugarpaste into an oval shape, then roll it between your two fingers to form the neck and the head. Gently pinch and stroke the other end to form a short tail.

4 Cut out a heart from some thinly rolled-out white sugarpaste and stick on the body for a tummy. Use fine sharp-pointed scissors (with points towards the feet of the Owl) to snip through the surface of the paste on the tummy to form lots of little spikes. Stroke the spikes downwards to look like feathers. When snipping with the scissors the underneath colour will then show.

5 Attach the wings to the sides of the body.

6 To make the face, roll out white paste thinly. Cut out a 2cm (³/₄in) and a 1cm (³/₈in) circle. Cut each circle into quarters, attach one of the larger quarters for the chin and mark with the Dresden tool to suggest feathers. For the eye area, roll out some pale brown paste. Cut out a 2cm (³/₄in) circle and cut it into quarters. Stick two of the small white quarters to the pale brown ones. Stick on two small eyes made from two balls of black sugarpaste. Attach these two quarters and a plain quarter for the forehead, to the face. Mark the forehead with lines radiating outwards using the Dresden tool.

7 Attach the tiny brown beak.

8 Make two small pieces of white fluff by pressing some sugarpaste through a sieve, sugarcraft gun, or garlic press. Stick it on to the head to look like 'ears'.

As Wise as an Owl

Try using white sugarpaste instead of chocolate brown. When rolling out the paste for the tummy feathers, roll out white and pale brown, press together and roll again. Cut out the heart shape and stick to the tummy with the pale brown stuck to the body. When snipping with the scissors, the colour will then show.

Macaw

Materials:

25g (just under 1oz) red sugarpaste

Small amount of yellow, orange, blue and black sugarpaste

Thin chocolate biscuit stick or candy stick for branch

Tools:

Sharp knife

Small sharp-pointed scissors

Dresden tool/ cocktail stick

Heart cutter: 1.25cm (½in)

Instructions:

1 To make the feet, roll two small pea-sized balls of orange sugarpaste and model into small carrot shapes. Cut the pointed end into three toes or claws for the feet. Attach to the 'branch' (chocolate biscuit/candy stick).

2 For the wings take a large pea-sized amount of red, a smaller ball of blue and a tiny ball of yellow sugarpaste.

Press them all together to form a cone shape with the blue paste at the tip of the wing. Mark on the lines for feathers using the Dresden tool, and store them in a plastic bag to keep them soft until needed.

16

3 To make the body, roll the rest of the red paste to a pointed cone approximately 8cm (3in) long. Roll the cone between two fingers at the wide end to form a neck and a head. Bend the body to stand it up, and mark on the lines for the tail feathers with the Dresden tool.

4 Roll out some yellow sugarpaste thinly to make the face. Cut out a 1.25cm (½in) heart and attach two tiny black sugarpaste balls for the eyes. Make two very thin strands of black sugarpaste and stick them to the yellow heart around the eyes. Cut the heart in half down the middle, and attach it to the head, leaving a small space in between for the beak.

5 For the beak, take a small pea-sized piece of yellow sugarpaste, and shape it to a fat cone. Make a smaller black cone and stick it under the yellow cone. Shape it to a curved beak and attach it to the front of the face.

6 Attach the wings to the body.

7 Dampen the tops of the feet and sit the Macaw on top.

The Real Macaw

For a totally tropical cake topper, model these colourful parrots. You could make the body in blue and the tip of the wings in red as a variation.

Mallard

Materials:

10g (¹/₃oz) brown sugarpaste

Small amounts of grey, orange, green, white, black and blue sugarpaste

Tools:

Wing mould

Dresden tool/ cocktail stick

Instructions:

1 To make the body, form a 5cm (2in) long cone of brown sugarpaste.

2 For the wings, place a tiny piece of blue sugarpaste at the tip of the wing feathers in the mould before putting in the grey sugarpaste. Stick the wings in place.

3 Take a small pea-sized ball of white sugarpaste and flatten slightly to make the collar. Stick on to the body.

4 For the head, roll a large pea-sized ball of green sugarpaste and stick it on top of the white collar. Attach tiny black eyes made from tiny balls of black sugarpaste.

5 To form the beak, roll a very small sausage of orange paste 1cm (³/₈in) long. Dampen the front of the face and lay the orange sausage vertically. Press the middle of the beak inwards, folding it in the middle. Gently curl up the end of the top beak and mark two tiny nostrils where the beak joins the face.

Simply Quackers!
*To make a female mallard, mix brown
and pale brown sugarpaste together,
and deliberately leave the colours mixed
with blotches of colour.*

Pelican

Materials:

25g (just under 1oz) white sugarpaste

Small amounts of orange, blue and black sugarpaste

Tools:

Dresden tool/ cocktail stick

Sharp knife

Instructions:

1 Make a small fish shape from the blue sugarpaste and store it in a plastic sandwich bag until it is needed to insert into the beak.

2 To make the feet, take two large pea-sized pieces of orange paste. Shape each to a cone 2cm (¾in) long, flatten slightly and mark them both with the Dresden tool to form three toes or claws.

3 For the wings, take two large pea-sized amounts of white sugarpaste, shape each to a cone 2cm (¾in) long, and shape a small pea-sized piece of black sugarpaste to a cone. Stick the black to the pointed tip of the wing. Mark on some simple feathers with the Dresden tool.

4 To make the body, shape some white sugarpaste to a pointed cone 6cm (2½in) long. Roll the fat end to form the long neck. The total length of the neck and body should be approximately 9cm (3½in).

5 Press the white sugarpaste with your finger to make a flat end where the beak will go.

6 Next, bend the whole neck backwards over the body and incline the head end forward.

7 For the beak, roll a large pea-sized piece of orange paste, 1.5cm (½in), to a cone, 2cm (¾in) long. Attach it to the front of the head. Make a cut with the sharp-pointed scissors from the point to make a narrow top beak and a bigger lower beak. Open the tip of the beak and place the small sugarpaste fish inside.

8 Make two tiny balls of black sugarpaste for the eyes and attach them to the side of the Pelican's head.

Gone Fishing

This sweet sugarpaste Pelican is perfect for someone special who loves to fish as much as this coastal bird.

Ostrich

Materials:

Three white edible sugar candy sticks

10g (¹/₃oz) black modelling paste (see page 6)

25g (just under 1oz) green modelling paste (see page 6)

Small amounts of peach, white, black and orange sugarpaste

Tools:

Small sieve/sugarcraft gun

Dresden tool/cocktail stick

Small sharp-pointed scissors

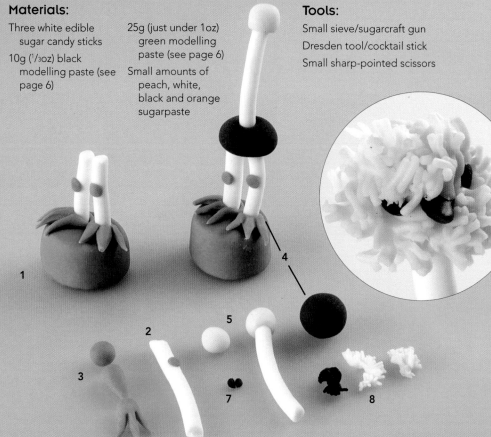

1

4

5

2

3

7

8

Instructions:

1 Mould the green modelling paste to a drum shape for the base.

2 For the legs, use two edible sugar candy sticks. Stick a very small ball of orange paste two-thirds along each stick and flatten it slightly.

3 To make the feet, take two pea-sized pieces of orange sugarpaste and shape each to a small pointed cone. Cut through the pointed end of each twice to form three toes or claws. Attach the feet to the top of the green drum base. Push the legs straight down through the back of the feet until the stick touches the surface.

4 For the body, form the black modelling paste into a ball. Dampen the tops of the legs and push the body on, making sure it is vertical.

5 To make the head, attach a large pea-sized piece of peach sugarpaste to a sugar candy stick. Dampen the other end of the stick and carefully push it straight in to the body.

6 The beak is made from a very small cone of black sugarpaste which has been slightly flattened. This is then attached to the front of the head.

7 For the eyes, cut a tiny ball of black paste in half to make two pointed oval eyes. Stick them on to the face in line with the beak.

8 To make 'fluff', push small amounts of soft sugarpaste through a sieve or a sugarcraft gun. Attach it to the dampened head and body, pushing it into place with point of the Dresden tool or a cocktail stick (don't press this on with your fingers as this could flatten it). The head should be peach all over, carefully avoiding the eyes and beak. The body should be black all over, and white around the base of the neck, with two little bits of white on each side for the tips of the wings.

Big Bird

I get lots of inspiration from toys and this big bird is modelled on those figures that wiggle when you push up from the base. It makes a quirky and hilarious cake topper.

Robin

Materials:

25g (just under 1oz) brown or chocolate sugarpaste

Small amounts of red, white and black sugarpaste

Tools:

Heart cutter: 2.5cm (1in)

Dresden tool/ cocktail stick

No. 2 piping tube

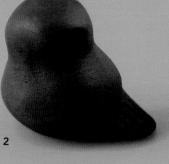

2

3

1
1

4

5   6

Instructions:

1 Make two wings from two small pea-sized pieces of the brown sugarpaste rolled into cones. Mark with the Dresden tool for the feathers.

2 For the body, shape a pointed cone, 6cm (2½in) long, from brown sugarpaste. Roll the wide end gently between your two fingers to form a short, fat neck. Stand the model up by bending the tail back. Mark the feathers on the tail with the Dresden tool.

3 Cut out a white heart from some rolled-out white paste. Attach it to the body, point down.

4 Cut out a red heart from some rolled-out red paste. Cut the pointed end off with the pointed end of the heart cutter. Attach it upside down, above the white heart, overlapping.

5 Push the piping tube into the red heart on the head to form eye sockets. Make tiny eyes from balls of black sugarpaste and stick them into the eye sockets.

6 Make a tiny pointed beak from black sugarpaste and stick it in place.

7 Attach the wings.

Rocking Robin!

You're sure to be rocking around the Christmas tree with these two cuties on your cake!

To make a more festive feathered friend, mark a line down the centre of the red heart, then mark on buttons with the piping tube. Make a cone of red paste and hollow the fat end slightly with your finger and thumb. Attach it to the top of the head and bend the point over to one side. Make white 'fluff' by pushing small amounts of sugarpaste through a sieve/sugarcraft gun. Attach the 'fluff' around the base of the hat, and on the point of the hat to make a bobble.

Green Woodpecker

Materials:

25g (just under1oz) pale green
  sugarpaste

Small amounts of darker green
  and red sugarpaste

Small amount of black
  modelling paste (see page 6)

Tools:

Dresden tool/
  cocktail stick

Instructions:

1 To make the body, roll the pale green sugarpaste to a pointed cone
approximately 8cm (3in) long. Roll it between your two fingers to form the
neck at the rounded end, and shape it so that the head is up and the body
and tail are straight. Mark some feathers on the tail with the Dresden tool.

2 For the wings, roll two large pea-sized pieces of darker green sugarpaste
into carrot shapes, each 4cm (1½in) long. Flatten them slightly and mark the
feathers on the wings with the Dresden tool. Attach them to the body.

3 To make the beak and mask, form some black modelling paste into a 3cm (1¼in) long cone. At the fat end, make a cut to form a 'Y' and shape the cut ends to form points, keeping the total length at 3cm (1¼in). Dampen inside the top of the 'Y' and stick it to the front of head, smoothing the side pieces in to look like a mask, with the point forming the beak.

4 Make two tiny balls each of white and black sugarpaste for the eyes. Stick the black on top of the white, and then attach them to the mask.

5 Make a small pea-sized ball of red sugarpaste, then shape and flatten it to a long, slightly rounded triangle. Attach on to the top of the head for the bird's crown.

Spotted Our Woodpecker?

To make a Spotted Woodpecker, make the body in white and the wings in black. Lay thin strips of white across the pointed ends of the wings for stripes and press in. Mark the feathers as before.

Turkey

Materials:

25g (just under 1oz) brown or chocolate sugarpaste

25g (just under 1oz) red modelling paste (see page 6)

Small amounts of red, orange, blue and black sugarpaste

Tools:

Circle cutters: 6cm (2½in), 4.5cm (1¾in), 3.5cm (1½in)

Heart cutter: 1cm (³/₈in)

Dresden tool/cocktail stick

Wing mould

Cocktail stick

Instructions:

1 To make the tail, roll out red, orange and brown sugarpaste to about 3–4mm (¹/₈in) thick. Cut out the three circles – the largest in red paste, the medium in orange and the smallest in brown. Stick the circles on top of each other and cut off one end as shown. Drag the Dresden tool from the outer edge to the base repeatedly, forming a fan shape. Stand the tail up on its cut edge, curving it backwards.

2 Model two wings using brown sugarpaste. You can either use the wing mould or model them by hand: shape two small pea-sized pieces of sugarpaste into long cones and flatten them slightly. Mark on the feathers.

3 Shape the rest of the brown sugarpaste for the head and body by rolling one end of the ball of paste with your fingers to 5cm (2in) long. The neck should be approximately the same length as the fat body. Bend the neck up sharply to an 'S' shape.

28

4 To make the face, roll out the blue sugarpaste thinly and cut out a small heart. Stick it on to the front of the neck. Roll out some red sugarpaste thinly. Cut out the same size heart and mark a line down the centre. Attach it under the blue heart, point side up.

5 To make the eyes, take two tiny white balls of sugarpaste, and stick two tiny black sugarpaste balls to them. Stick them on to the blue face.

6 Roll a tiny brown pointed cone of sugarpaste for the beak. Stick it on, and mark on the nostrils with a cocktail stick. Roll a tiny strand of red paste and attach above the beak, positioning it so that it hangs down on one side.

7 Attach the body to the front of the tail, and stick the wings on to the sides of the body, with the tips of the wings pointing down.

Dove Story

Make this fantail dove in the same way as the Turkey, but model the body in white sugarpaste and the beak in pink paste. Don't make the face parts, but for each eye make one tiny pink sugarpaste ball and one in black. Cut them in half to make pointed oval eyes, and attach the wings pointing down.

Peacock

Materials:

10g (¹/₃oz) blue
  sugarpaste

10g (¹/₃oz) green
  modelling paste
  (see page 6)

Small amounts of blue,
  dark blue, black and
  white modelling paste
  (see page 6)

Small amount of edible
  wafer paper

Tools:

Garrett frill cutter

Cutting wheel/knife

Dresden tool/
  cocktail stick

Circle cutter: 0.5cm (¼in)

Sharp-pointed scissors

Instructions:

1 For the tail, roll out green
modelling paste to 2mm
(¹/₁₆in) thick. Cut out a garrett
frill and cut straight across
at one end. Mark on the
feathers by dragging the
curved part of the Dresden
tool over the paste. Cut out
holes with the circle cutter to
represent the design on the
feathers. Roll out blue and
dark blue sugarpaste and cut
out circles to stick on to the
tailpiece as shown. Allow it
to dry flat overnight, turning
it over occasionally to make
sure it dries evenly all over.

2 Roll the rest of the blue
sugarpaste between your
two fingers to make a 'skittle'
shape for the head and body.

3 For the face, make a tiny
pointed beak from black
sugarpaste and stick it on.
To make the eyes, take a tiny
ball of white and another of
black sugarpaste, and stick

them together. Cut across them to make two pointed oval eyes and attach them to the head.

4 To make the crown, cut out a small triangle, 1cm (³/₈in) long, of edible wafer paper. Cut it with scissors to make one fringed edge. Stick the pointed end into the top of the head.

5 Carefully raise the tail section and attach it to the body, ensuring that the whole bird will stand up on its own.

Proud as a Peacock

That's how you'll be feeling when you unveil your majestic sugar masterpieces. This Peacock will add glamour to the plainest of gateaux. It is also stunning made all in white.

Eagle

Materials:

25g (just under 1oz) brown or chocolate sugarpaste

Small amounts of white, pale orange and black sugarpaste

Edible wafer paper

Food colour felt tip pen: brown

Edible powder colour: brown

Tools:

Dusting brush

Dresden tool/ cocktail stick

Sharp knife

Template

Instructions:

1 Using the wing template, trace the wing pattern on to edible wafer paper with the felt tip pen – make two. Carefully cut out the wings. Make the same marks to suggest feathers using the felt tip pen on both sides of each of the wings. Brush the brown edible powder colour from the edge of the wing inwards.

2 To make the body, form some brown sugarpaste into a cone. Attach a large pea-sized piece of white sugarpaste to the large end for the head. Use the tip of the Dresden tool to drag the surface of the two colours together forming a smooth feathered join. Continue to lengthen the cone shape to 8cm (3in), slightly thinner for the head and longer at the tail end. Bend the body to stand it up and shape and curve the head.

3 For the beak, shape a small piece of pale orange sugarpaste to a short pointed cone. Attach it to the head, curve the tip over and mark in the nostrils.

4 Make the eyes by rolling a tiny ball of black sugarpaste, and cut it in half to make two pointed ovals. Stick them on to the head.

5 To model the feet, shape two small cones of pale orange sugarpaste. Cut the pointed ends to make three toes or claws on each. Attach them under the body.

6 Dampen the back of the eagle and attach the wings.

Bird's Eye View

Keep your eagle eye out for this big bird – with edible wafer paper wings, he's sure to fly off your guests' plates!

Flamingo

Materials:

Three pink edible sugar candy sticks

25g (just under 1oz) blue modelling paste

25g (just under 1oz) pink modelling paste (see page 6)

Small amounts of yellow and black sugarpaste

Tools:

Wing mould

Sharp knife/scissors

Instructions:

1 To make the base, shape the blue paste to a drum shape.

2 Make two small cones of pink sugarpaste and flatten slightly for the feet. Cut out two tiny triangles from the wide end of the cones, and mark two lines to form three toes or claws. Stick one foot on top of the base, and push in one candy stick for the leg. Dampen the middle of the leg and wrap a thin sausage of pink paste around it for the knee.

3 Cut the second candy stick diagonally across the middle. Dampen one of the flat ends and attach it to the second foot. Dampen the two diagonal cut edges and stick on a small ball of pink paste to form a knee joint.

4 Form two slightly larger than pea-sized pieces of pink sugarpaste, and attach to each end of the third candy stick for the head and body. Dampen the top of the first leg and push the body on top, keeping the neck vertical.

5 Dampen the top of the bent second leg and push it into the side of the body. Also dampen the side of the straight knee to stick the bent leg to it for extra support. Leave it to dry for a few hours.

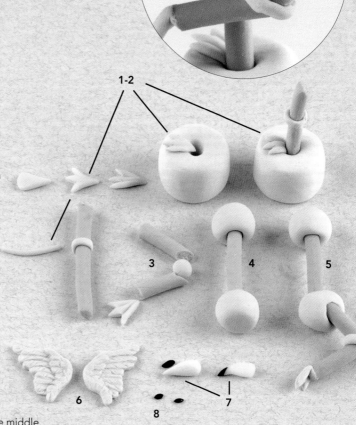

6 Make at least two pairs of wings from the mould in pink paste. Attach one pair from the front of the tummy, hiding the body. Attach the second pair over the back, with the tips of the feathers pointing downwards, forming the tail.

7 Form the beak from a small pea-sized piece of yellow paste, shaped into a pointed cone. Attach a tiny piece of black paste at the pointed end. Attach the beak to the head, curve the beak down and mark on two nostrils.

8 Make the eyes out of two tiny balls of black paste.

In the Pink

Make this sugar Flamingo and he will proudly balance atop your cake on one leg without so much as a wobble!

Cockatoo

Materials:

25g (just under 1oz)
  white sugarpaste

Small amounts of
  yellow, grey and
  black sugarpaste

Edible wafer paper

Chocolate stick
  or candy stick
  for branch

Tools:

Wing template

Dresden tool/cocktail stick

Sharp knife/scissors

No. 2 piping tube

Template

Instructions:

1 Trace the wings on to the edible wafer paper using the template. Use the Dresden tool to keep the wafer paper white. Cut out the wings with scissors.

2 For the body, make an 8cm (3in) cone out of white sugarpaste. Roll the fat end between your two fingers to make the neck and the head. Mark on the tail feathers with the Dresden tool or a cocktail stick.

3 Make the beak out of a short cone of grey sugarpaste, attach it to the head and curve downwards. Mark on the two nostrils.

4 Make the eye sockets by pushing the piping tube into the sugarpaste head. Make two tiny balls of black sugarpaste and stick them into the eye sockets.

5 Shape a short cone of yellow sugarpaste for the crest. Cut into the pointed end, making at least three cuts. Attach it to the top of the head and curve the points upwards.

6 Make the feet from two small grey cones of sugarpaste. Cut the pointed end twice to form three toes or claws. Attach the feet to the candy stick, close together. Dampen the top of the feet and sit the body on top.

7 Dampen the sides of the body and attach the wings.

Spread Your Wings

Try your hand at modelling this popular pet in sugarpaste – no birdcage required!

Rooster

Materials:

White edible sugar
   candy stick

25g (just under 1oz) black
   modelling paste (see
   page 6)

Small amounts of red,
   green, orange, purple
   and black modelling
   paste (see page 6)

10g (1/3oz) purple
   sugarpaste

5g (1/6oz) yellow sugarpaste

Tools:

Sharp-pointed scissors

Dresden tool/cocktail stick

Edible sugar candy stick to
   use for modelling

Instructions:

1 For the tail feathers, roll some small
pea-sized balls of the red, green and
purple modelling paste. Form each of
them into a thin cone approximately
2cm (¾in) long. Dampen the fat ends
and press gently together with the tips
fanning out. Curve the tips all in the
same direction. Leave to dry for a
few hours.

2 To make the base, form a fat
cube of the black paste. Make
a hole in the centre of the cube
using the dry candy stick and
remove it.

3 Make six very thin, tiny cones of orange
sugarpaste for the feet. Stick them to the
top of the base.

4 For the body, form a pointed oval of purple
sugarpaste 5cm (2in) long. Dampen the surface and
lay a candy stick across the centre. Fold the purple
sugarpaste in half, bringing the points together and keeping
the candy stick stuck inside, with each end sticking out of the paste.
Curve the pointed end upwards for the tail.

5 To make the head, shape the yellow sugarpaste to a sausage 3cm (1¼in) long. Insert a dry candy stick lengthwise, almost to the end and then remove the stick. Pinch out the open end to widen it. Cut into the widened edge with scissors to make a zigzag edge. Dampen the inside edge of the paste and attach the head to the body over the stick. Make two small eyes from the black sugarpaste and stick them on. Flatten a 1cm (³/₈in) sausage of red sugarpaste, dampen along the top of the head, attach the red paste and make indentations with the Dresden tool or a cocktail stick for the Rooster's comb.

6 Stick a very small orange cone on for the beak and cut across the middle with scissors to open it. Make two very small thin cones of red paste and attach them to the front of the face, just under the beak.

7 Dampen the candy stick and push the Rooster into the base, making sure it's vertical.

8 For the wings, take two pea-sized pieces of purple sugarpaste and shape each into a cone, flatten, and mark on feathers with the Dresden tool or cocktail stick. Dampen them and attach them to the body, leaving the tips of the wings slightly apart. Dampen the base of the tail feathers and press them between the tips of the wings to attach them.

Cock-a-Doodle-Doo!

Wakey wakey! It's time to start sugarcrafting this farmyard favourite! Use more earthy shades of sugarpaste for the body, wings and tail, and lose the red comb and wattle to make a brood of hens to join your Rooster.

Lovebirds

Materials:

10g (¹⁄₃oz) green sugarpaste

Small amounts of yellow,
orange, red, black and
white sugarpaste

Tools:

Dresden tool/cocktail stick

No. 2 piping tube

2

4

3

Instructions:

1 For the wings, take
a pea-sized amount of
green sugarpaste for
each wing and shape it
to a pointed cone. Mark
it with the Dresden tool
or a cocktail stick to look
like feathers.

2 To make the body,
attach a large pea-sized
piece of yellow and one of
orange sugarpaste to the ball
of green. Dampen if necessary.
Shape to a 6cm (2½in) cone, smoothing the joins
between the colours with your fingers. Roll the fat end
between your fingers to form a neck. Curve the body to
stand up and mark on the tail feathers with the Dresden
tool or a cocktail stick. Attach the wings.

1

3 Mark the eye sockets on to the head with a piping tube, and attach two tiny eyes using two balls of black sugarpaste.

4 Make an indentation where the beak will go. Shape a small, red pointed cone of sugarpaste and attach it to the head in the indentation. Curve the tip of the beak down and mark on the nostrils.

Birds of a Feather

These small African birds are renowned for showing affection to their mates, so spread the love with a little sugarpaste! These would be ideal for a cake celebrating an engagement or wedding anniversary.

Kingfisher

Materials:

25g (just under 1oz) blue
   sugarpaste

Small amounts of
   orange and white
   sugarpaste

Small amount of black
   modelling paste (see
   page 6)

Edible powder pearl
   colour: Glacier Blue

Tools:

Wing mould

Heart cutter: 2.5cm (1in)

Sharp-pointed scissors

Dusting brush

No. 2 piping tube

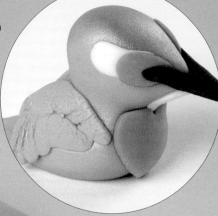

Instructions:

1 Make a pair of wings
in the mould, or shape
them by hand in blue
sugarpaste.

2 Form a 6cm (2½in)
cone-shaped body from
the blue sugarpaste.
Make the neck by rolling
the fat end between your two
fingers, and bend the body to
sit up. Shape the head to a slight
point and stroke the top of the
head to make it slightly flatter.
Attach the wings. Brush the
Kingfisher's body and wings with
the edible powder pearl colour.

3 Shape two 1.5cm (½in) long
white sugarpaste cones, and
two in orange, the same size. Stick
the orange on to the white, as shown. Flatten
them slightly and attach them to the head,
points forward.

4 For the chest, make another white sugarpaste cone 1.5cm (½in) long, flatten it slightly and attach it to the front of the Kingfisher. Roll out some orange sugarpaste and cut out a heart. Stick it on below the white oval.

5 To make the beak and mask, form some black modelling paste into a 2cm (¾in) long cone. Cut the fat end to form a 'Y', and shape the cut ends to form points – keep the total length at 2cm (¾in). Dampen the inside top of the 'Y' and stick to the front of the head, smoothing the side pieces in to look like a mask, with the point forming the beak. Mark on the eyes with a No. 2 piping tube.

Take the Plunge

Reach for your edible pearl colour powder to add a shimmer to this blue beauty of the bird world.

Swan

Materials:

25g (just under 1oz) white
   sugarpaste

5g (1/6oz) blue sugarpaste

Small amounts of orange and
   black sugarpaste

Tools:

Wing mould

Dresden tool

Cocktail stick

No. 2 piping tube

1

2

3

4

5

7

Instructions:

1 Shape 5g (1/4oz) of white sugarpaste into a short cone for the body. Curve the pointed end up for the tail.

2 Make a pair of white wings from the mould. Dampen them and attach them to the body with the wings touching each other on top of the body.

3 For the head and neck, roll a large pea-sized piece of white sugarpaste to a 6cm (2½in) sausage, leaving one end slightly fatter for the head.

4 Make a very small 1.5cm (½in) sausage of black paste for the mask. Roll the ends to form points and attach to the front of the head. Mark on the eyes with the no. 2 piping tube.

5 To make the beak, shape a 1cm (³/₈in) long cone of orange sugarpaste. Attach it to the front of the black mask and mark on the nostrils with a cocktail stick. Gently curve the tip of the beak upwards.

6 Dampen the front of the body and attach the base of the neck under the front, curving over the back, forming an 'S' shape with the head facing forwards.

7 Mix blue paste with some white, deliberately leaving it streaky. Make four long thin cones of this sugarpaste, curl the wide end inwards and attach the narrow ends together to form a swirl of 'water' for the swan to sit on. Stick the swan on top.

Swan Lake

Make this graceful waterbird for someone very special; the swan has long been a symbol of love, purity, beauty and partnership.

45

Hummingbird

Materials:

5g (1/6oz) purple sugarpaste

Small amount of black sugarpaste

Edible wafer paper

Edible powder colour: Deep Pink

Edible powder pearl colour: Frosty Holly

Food colour felt tip pen: purple

Tools:

Sharp-pointed scissors

Dusting brush

Sharp knife

No. 2 piping tube

Templates

Instructions:

1 On edible wafer paper, draw two wings and a beak with the food colour felt tip pen, using the templates provided. Carefully cut them out. Turn the wafer paper wings over and draw the wings on the other side. Brush the Hummingbird's beak and wings with the dry edible powder colour in Deep Pink.

2 For the body, shape the purple sugarpaste to a 5cm (2in) long cone. Roll the wide end between your two fingers to form the neck, and cut out a 'V' shape for the tail. Bend the body to stand it up. With sharp-pointed scissors, mark two short vertical lines into the back for the wings and a short vertical line for the beak. Mark on two holes for the eye sockets using the no. 2 piping tube.

3 Brush edible powder pearl colour in Frosty Holly over the body.

4 Make two tiny eyes from black sugarpaste, dampen the eye sockets and stick them on.

5 Very lightly dampen the scissor-marks and insert the beak and the wings.

This is Sure to Take Off

Try using different brightly-coloured sugarpaste and coloured pearl powders; such as blue sugarpaste with lilac pearl powder, red sugarpaste with gold powder or green sugarpaste with pink pearl powder. The shimmer really lifts your sugar creations.

Acknowledgements

To my husband Mike, who constantly looked after me and made
sure I was fed while I was concentrating on the book.   .
With many thanks to Anne Killick for all her help.
I would also like to thank the staff at Search Press who created
the book: Roz Dace for commissioning the book,
Alison Shaw for editing, Debbie Patterson for the photography,
Marrianne Mercer for the design and Jeff Boatwright for production.

Publisher's Note

If you would like more information about sugarcraft,
try *Sugar Animals*, Search Press, 2009; *Decorated Cup Cakes*,
Search Press, 2009 or *Sugar Fairies*, Search Press, 2010
all by Frances McNaughton.

You are invited to visit the
author's website
www.franklysweet.co.uk